a little smoke

poems by Bill Gainer

Spartan Press

Spartan Press
Kansas City, Missouri

Copyright © Bill Gainer, 2024
First Edition: 1 3 5 7 9 10 8 6 4 2
ISBN: 978-1-958182-89-5
LCCN: 2024946238
Cover image: Bill Gainer
Author photo: Unknown

All rights reserved. No part of this publication may be reproduced or transmitted in any form or by any means, electronic or mechanical, including photocopying, recording or by info retrieval system, without prior written permission from the author.

Acknowledgements:

Special thanks to Jason Ryberg, Eva West, Todd Cirillo, and the editors of these publications:

Ariel Chart, Poems for All, River Dog Zine #1, The Rye Whiskey Review, Polarity, Moms 4 Housing, Ted Ate America, The Canary, Red Fez, The BeZine, Medusa's Kitchen, Scattergun Poetry, Red Fez, Journal, Americans and Other – an anthology of international poets, Tule Review, Lummox 9, Redshift #4, Thought for Food, The Canary, Rusty Truck, Gasconade Review #6, Slaves and Bulldozers, Cultural Weekly, Lummox 8, Bold Monkey, Heroin Love Songs, Bold Monkey, Last Call Chinaski, River Dog Zine #1, Guerrilla Genesis Press, Issue 27, Cultural Weekly, Scattergun Poetry Journal, Chiron Review.

A True Story. Spartan Press, 2021.

Table of Contents

Mrs. Parker / 1

To Iris with Love / 3

A Lonely Day Long Ago / 4

What I Think / 5

The Anonymous Poem / 6

She Likes a House Full / 7

Unrealized Perfection / 8

The Mexicans / 9

The Music / 10

The Yellow Bird / 11

The Quiet / 12

The Woman I Live With / 13

Making Rent / 14

To Be Old / 15

Screaming at the Moon / 16

The Brotherhood of the Street / 17

From the Girl who Sees Things / 18

The Reason Old Men Shuffle / 19

Little Monsters / 20

Sausage, Eggs and Toast / 21

An All American Cat / 23

Last Night's Traffic Stop / 24

Collecting Scars / 26

Date Night / 27

Mexican Bob / 28

A Hot Tuesday Afternoon / 30

A Death in the Family / 31

A Bit of a Confession) / 32

Someday, Maybe / 33
The Watsonville Job / 34
The Color of Paint / 35
Gifts from Bela Lugosi / 36
"Truth, Justice and the American Way" / 37
You Never Know / 38
We Talked about Things – it didn't Help / 39
Frank's Luck / 40
Molly's Funeral / 41
To the Stars / 42
The Life and Times of an Iguana / 43
The Taste of Neon / 44
How I Park My Car / 45
How a Hitman Eats Spaghett / 46
Where Things Battle for their Lives / 47
The Scales of Worth / 48
Me and the Moon / 49
A Portrait of a Dear Friend / 50
The Collar / 51
Nature's Child / 52
Needing Wishes / 53
If Only / 54
A Tip for Hard Times / 55
Death of a Swing Set / 56
It was the 1950s / 57
Concerns for a Spider / 58
The Work of Trees / 59
An Oddity / 60
Counting Monsters / 63
Unfriended Again / 64

Still Loving Somebody – You / 65
Sunrise on a Blind Alley / 66
A Dependable Friend / 67
Ambitious Young Men / 68
Wishing on a Monarch / 69
A Late Night Report / 70
Then and Now / 72
Private Dreams / 74
Searching for Two, Finding Three / 75
Another Tomorrow / 76
Keeping Dogs / 77
We Get By / 78
Trying for Human / 79
Filling Time and Gone / 81
Scary People and Madmen / 82
Sunday's Family Potluck / 83
Sub-Allergies / 84
Private Things / 85
The Wait / 87
Reporting Secrets / 88
From My Hands to Yours / 89
A Wish for a Friend on Her Birthday / 90
Dark Skies, Turkey Vultures … / 91
Another Goodbye / 93
Heart-worn / 94
To Dance / 96
How I Heard It / 98
Dust Bowl Photos / 99
Walking into Loneliness / 101
Old Poets / 103

Different Kinds of Friends / 104
The Lucky One / 106
Bloody August / 107
Dressing for Drinks and a Movie / 108
Realizing Brautigan / 109
Traveling with Ghosts / 110
Shaky Old Men and Upscale Joints / 111
The Purpose of the Little Garage / 112
Amazing Things about Bugs / 114
Drinking with Saints / 115
A Place to Suffocate / 117
Gardening by Starlight / 118
Moving Out / 120
The Imposition of Guilt / 121
A New Used Hat / 122
The Truth about Love Stories / 124
A Little Something for the Dogs / 125
When Love Died / 126
Disneyland Vacation Summary / 127
Don Quixote's Last Battle / 128
Jane – even after she went crazy / 129
Once We Were Kids / 130
Never Less than Harmful / 132
Finding Forever / 133
You're Dead / 134
A Friend Reads Siddhartha / 135
Once at the Edge of the Ocean / 136
The Distance Between Us / 137
Falling Stars / 138
Learning to Fly / 139

Believing in a Troubled God / 140
Dogs and Reptiles / 141
In Dust and Ash / 142
Lighting Cigarettes and Saying No / 143
Thinking about Stuff / 144
Miles Away / 145
The Lockdown / 146
Happily Ever After / 147
The Stranger / 148
What People Eat / 149
Lying to the Bill Collector / 150
The Focused Beatle / 151
Breakfast / 152
The Truth about Wild Dogs / 153
The Art of Growing Cacti / 155
Waiting for the Rain / 156
Counting Kills / 157
A Quick Turnaround / 158
A Drive to the Coast / 159
A Lonely Angel / 160
The Package / 161
For the Boy / 163
Five Love Letters / 164
The American Poem / 166
The Girl with Long Fingers / 167
At Almost 75 / 168
The Movies / 169
She can Fix an Ocean / 170
A Little Smoke / 171
Mexico / 172

For Neeli Cherkovski

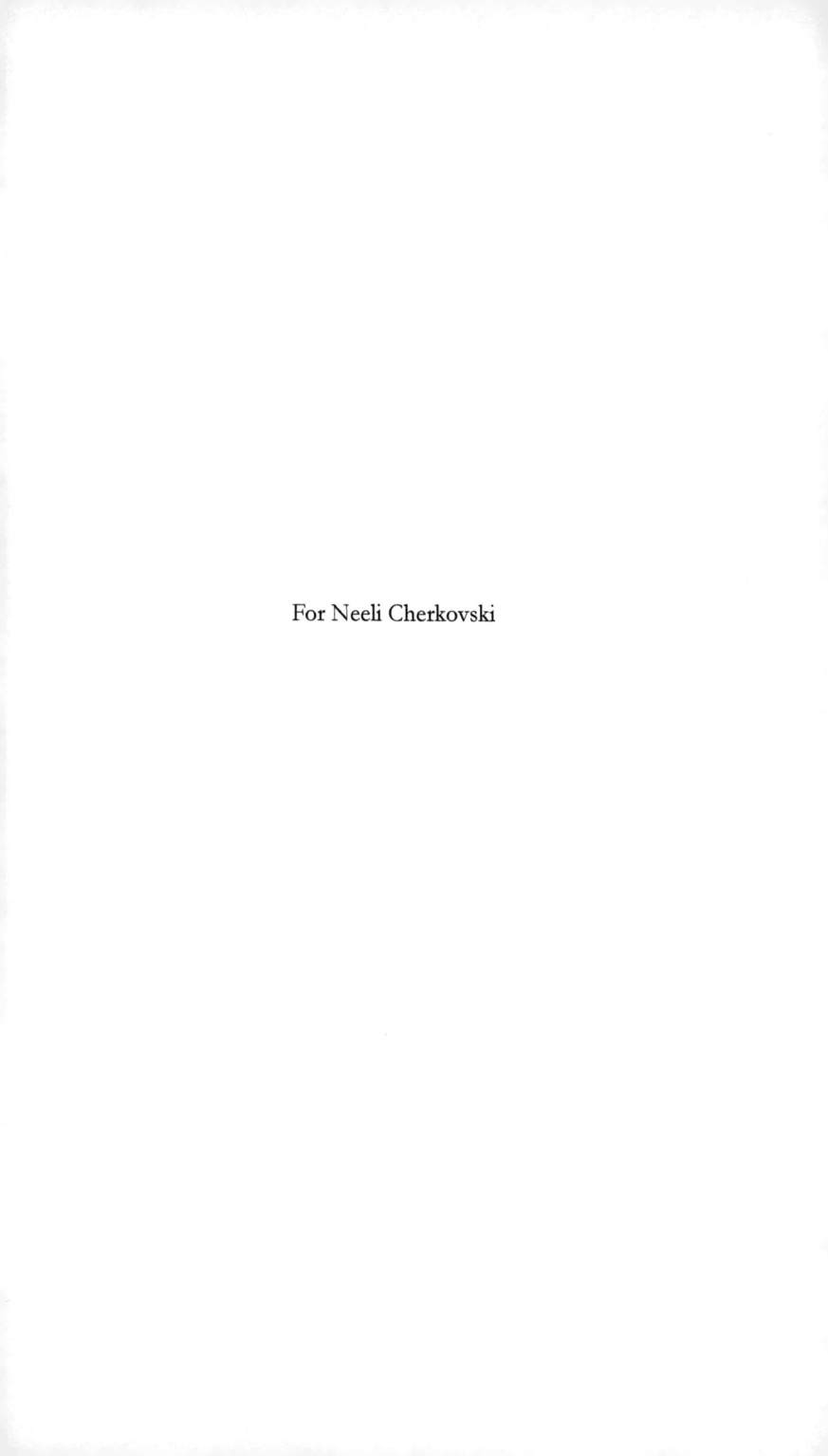

A little smoke

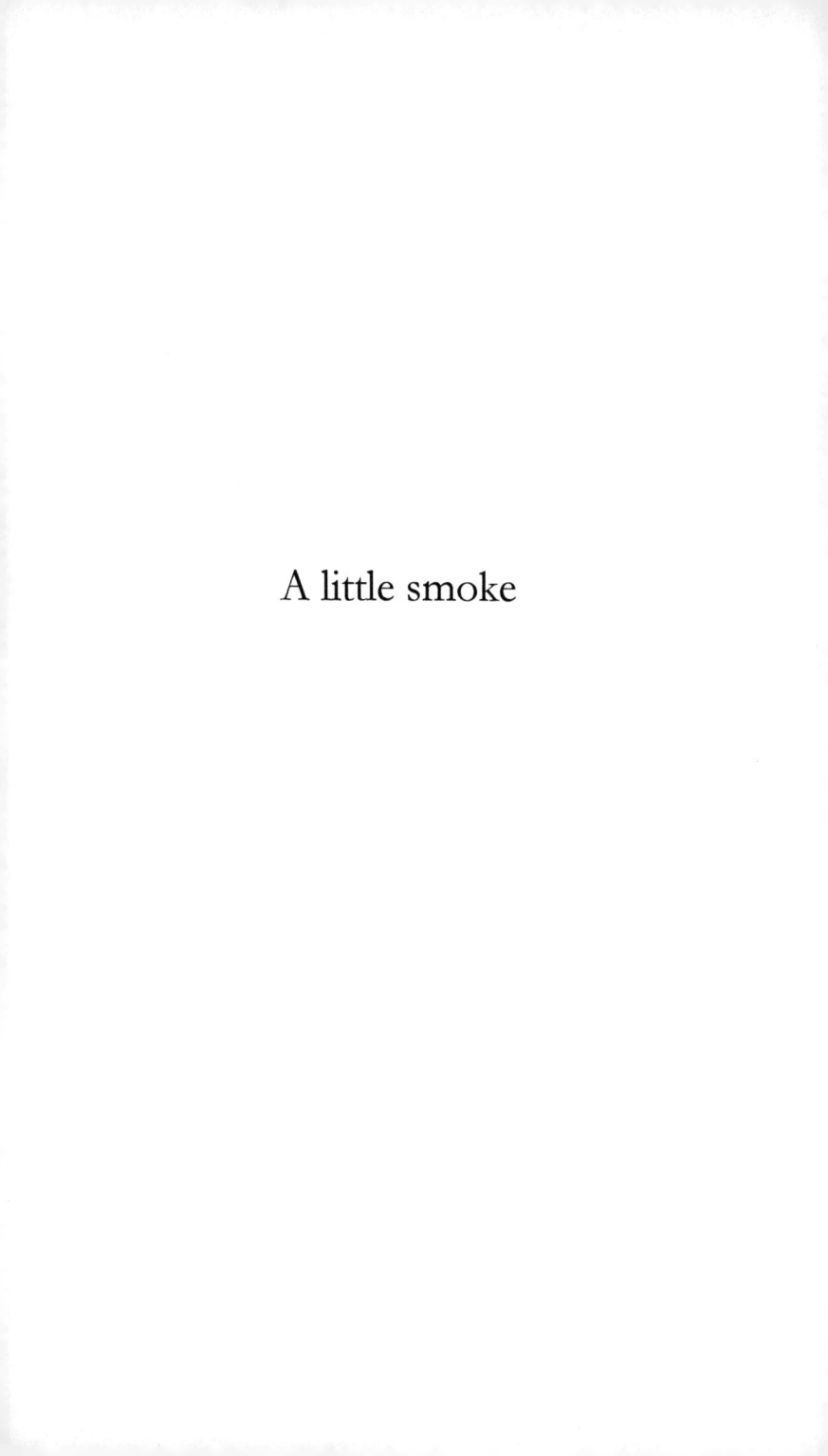

Mrs. Parker

School –
third grade
long ago.
Not my place.

Me trying to be
invisible
she asked
*where do stars
come from*
called my name.

Burn barrels.
Some of the kids
rolled their eyes
others covered
their faces – both hands
peeked through the cracks
between fingers
laughed.

Why burn barrels?

*Because sparks
need to be free
to rise up
and find their place
in the sky –
become stars.
I will too
someday.*

On the way to recess
she called me to her desk

looked into my face
and with serious eyes
said
I believe you —

pointed to the door
motioned
for me to go.

To Iris with Love

for Iris Reinhardt

I've grown
accustomed
to saying yes,
but today –
no.

Don't go –
please –
stay a little longer.

The days seem
so much warmer
with you in them.

I know the pain
has pushed
and pills
prescribed –
you need to go.

But still
no –
I won't say goodbye –
ever …
        Not to you.

A Lonely Day Long Ago

How lonely.
An empty
schoolyard
on an overcast
late winter's
afternoon.

Everyone's home
warm.
Even the
tether ball
is inside
out of the cold.

What I Think

The greatest sin
has to be
allowing some
a simple death ...

The Anonymous Poem

Tonight –
that's all I got.
Six lines
of a skinny poem,
not even
a title.

She likes a House Full

We have friends coming
tomorrow.
She likes a house full.
The joint
is clean
the yard
nice.
Been working
all day.
She wishes
the barber had time.
Says
you always look like
a crazy man.
Wants me to be nice.
I will.
Truth is
I'm just happy
to be
one of the guests.

Unrealized Perfection

There are many ways
to do a suicide.
Some so beautiful
nobody knows.

The Mexicans

Everybody's got a problem
some people two, three
maybe four.
I'm thinking the only folks
that can fix these
problems
are the Mexicans.
They fix everything.
And now
he's (Trump) pissed them off too.
This is not going to end well
not at all.
Not without
the Mexicans.

The Music

She reached over
dimmed the music
said, *I couldn't hear
you breathe.*

The Yellow Bird

That yellow bird –
it's not
from around here.
I've seen his kind before
but not him.
He's a stranger.
I can tell
by his accent.

The Quiet

The evening
cool
the girls
sleeping
and I'm here
with you.
Nothing out there
calls.
It's quiet time.
The lights in the back
on.
I can feel the breeze
your breath.
It's nice knowing
we share the night.

If today
no one's told you
they love you –
I do.

Yeah – It's you
and the evening
keeping love
keeping me
alive.

The Woman I Live With

She helped her dad
bury her mom.
Then buried
him
by herself.
My wish
is to be the last
of this work
she does
and that the kids
watching her
learn –
that saying goodbye
is a gentle business
and when it's
her time
I wish for them
to do the job
as softly
as she has.

Making Rent

It's nice
when
there's a bit of
color
in the booze.

It's the bartender
heavy handed
giving the boss
the finger.
Making his rent
on tips.

To Be Old

The nights
have learned
to shuffle
a handful of memory.

Time asks for you
no more
just waits.

Who cares
if it's
eggs and sausage
or a cool morning kiss.

The day is on you
the night's waiting.

I noticed you've started
ignoring
the red signal lights.
The danger
means nothing.

There must be
an easier way
to go
than growing old.

Screaming at the Moon

Too many fucking memories.
Too
goddamn many –
even for this old man
to carry.
If the gods loved me
they would have put a
bullet in what's left
a long time ago.
Instead
they cursed you
with time ...
It's a good night
to stand
out back,
look to the sky,
and scream –
fuck you –
fuck you –
JUST – FUCK YOU.
I know it scares
the neighbors ...
me too,
sometimes.

The Brotherhood of the Street

The guy walking
toward me
a bit scruffy
stops
asks
the guy kneeling
if he could be
next.

The guy
with the clippers
cutting hair
looks up
says
What you want man?

A trim.

*I'm trying to sell
these clippers.
You want to buy 'em?
Three bucks.
I keep the batteries.
You got any money?*

No.

Then fuck off.

From the Girl Who Sees Things
for Rhea Adri

She's interested
in what grows –
in abandoned gardens
of the graying city:

> *A spent 22 shell*
> *used for shooting*
> *rats.*
>
> *A torn fortune cookie*
> *reads –*
> *Don't Panic ...*
>
> *One house slipper*
> *only one.*
>
> *Other things*
> *dropped or blown*
> *waiting*
> *for the harvest.*

The Reason Old Men Shuffle

Murderer
yes, I know.
A lifetime spent
killing
invisible gods.

Who knew
there are so many?
Their corpses scattered
everywhere –
the reason old men
shuffle –

trying to avoid
tripping
but still
now and then
we do.

Little Monsters

If you hang out
in the yard long enough
the lizards
start watching
your every move.
It's fucking creepy.

Sausage, Eggs and Toast

Haven't been
sending out the poems
like I should.

Been working out back
probably harder
than someone my age
needs to –
it helps
to keep the meanness
down.
Yeah, in times like these
it's easy to have a
flare up
say things you shouldn't
do things you'll
regret
upset folks
you love.

Tomorrow
I'll drop
some shotgun shells
off at an old friend's
go out to the dump
ask about recycling paint.

Maybe stop, have lunch
read the paper.

If the guy is still fucking with

the moms and their babies
I'll probably be home
early
dig out in the back

till the lights come on
and Kae St. Marie calls out –
says dinner's ready
sausage, eggs and toast
come on in baby –
you've done all you can
for today.

An All American Cat

For Christ's sake
they shot the fireworks off –
right in front of the house.
Like it was just for me.
I'm not in the mood.
Too much crazy
going on these days.
They succeeded in scaring
the dogs
and now the cat's gone
missing.
Probably won't show up
for a couple of days.
I hope he eats
a little something
while he's out.
God bless America
and all that crap.
If you see the cat
let me know.

Last Night's Traffic Stop

Got pulled over
lights flashing
badge polished.
The cop –
a kid
wanting to know
if I knew why.

Nope.
He said,
33 in a 25.

There was a lecture:
focus
being safe
rules.

Looking to the heavens
I said
It's a Blood Moon –
son.
At almost seventy
I've never seen it
ever.
This is the first time
it's beautiful.

He let me off
with a warning.

Said in the future
pay more attention.

I will officer – I will.

Collecting Scars

Before the deep tissue
it's just a cut ...
after that
you'll probably need
stitches.
They got ways
to make it stop
bleeding ...
The rest –
you're on your own.

Date Night

We had red meat
tonight.
Prime Rib
and the other
stuff —
all the other
stuff.
14 ounces
we ate about ten
each
and the other
stuff —
all the other
stuff.
Took the rest
home
dogs
and sandwiches.
Our bloodlust
complete.

Mexican Bob

Half the people I know
change their names.
Nothing illegal
just goofy.

Me –
no.
Have thought about it
though.
Something strong
with teeth.
Call me –
"Mexican Bob."

Imagine
two days out
on one of those
hot, dusty, dry
Nevada Highways –
395
that's a good one –
top to bottom.

Pulling my rig
into one of those
nowhere joints.
Pushing the doors open –
slow.
The place goes silent.

A low voice
asks

who's that?

The bartender
boots nailed to the floor
frozen

whispers
why that
that's
"Mexican Bob."

A Hot Tuesday Afternoon

Sitting alone
watching a skinny
Puerto Rican girl
small breasts
dancing nasty
to Carlos Santana ...
told the bar maid
I'll have another
ask her to
play it again –
please.
And to split
the change
with the dancer.

A Death in the Family

Know this Ed,
your mom is the one person in the family
who has always been with me
and will continue to be
until I am no more.

My heart is breaking for you.
I know you were/are a good son,
a good man.
She always looked at you
with something special
in her eyes.
You've done the best
any son
can:
protected her,
made her safe, comfortable,
and above all –
loved her.

There is nothing more to give ...
no one is ever ready for this ...
ever.
Let me know if there is anything
I can do to help.
What I have is yours.

You and yours
are in my heart –
always will be.
Be blessed – Bill.

A Bit of a Confession
for Dale Pendell, 1946-2017

At Dale's memorial
there was a table of things
he had created
(made) in his time.
There was a bowl
of glass marbles.
They were beautiful.
I thought about stealing
one.
Didn't
but
there was
a moment ...
They
were beautiful ...

Someday, Maybe

I've never actually
kissed the moon

though it has
seduced me
on occasion.

A kiss
would be nice –
someday
maybe.

The Watsonville Job. '69 – '80

Worked for an outfit
over in Watsonville
years ago.
Three kids
a wife
and a house payment.
They gave us a turkey
and a ham,
Thanksgiving and Christmas –
eleven years on the job.

I'd give the tickets
to Kae St. Marie
she'd go over
to the little grocery
in Pajaro
CA
pick out
what was right
for us
write the boss
a thank you note
invite him over.
He never showed.

We ate good –
all the way down to
the carcass boiling
for late night soup ...

The Color of Paint

Painted the shed
a deep forestry brown
so in the dark
it disappears.

Tonight, it's gone.

If this works
as planned
in the morning
it will be returned.

If not
we lost
another one.

Gifts from Bela Lugosi

Thought I saw it
asked.
She said
a goddamn bat
get it.
Rose and Mrs. Menebroker
the dogs
thought it was
great fun
bouncing on the bed
too short
to get any altitude.
I broke the upstairs'
window screen
getting it off –
hurrying
the little bastard's
escape.
He shit on the wall
on the way out.

"Truth, Justice and the American Way."
the day Kavanaugh got the job, 10.6.2018

I've been in this fight
too many years —
all losing does
is tell me
I'm on the right side ...
Tonight,
I'll sit in the back
alone,
tell myself to rise up.
The fight ain't over —
you're still in it ...
and I am too...

You Never Know

The kid in line
looked shifty.
I didn't trust him.

Asked me to sign
his book.
I figured he was –
up to
something.

These days
things happen.
You never know.

No sense
taking a chance.
I forged
my name.

We Talked about Things – it didn't Help

My barber's wife
is dying.
It was the saddest
haircut
ever.

Frank's Luck

Back in the day
there were burn barrels
up and down the block
in every backyard.
The old men in their
T-shirts, coveralls
heavy jackets
depending on the season
rain or shine
would fire 'em up
midday
Sunday.
Gather around
drink beer
mostly
wine
if they had to.
Talk about the ballgame
the Saturday night fights
and Frank's luck
at Friday night's
card game.
That's how it used to be
on Sundays
when the women
were at church.

Molly's Funeral

I'll sit in the car
wait for you.
Sip a little bourbon
take a little
nap.
We'll drive home
slow
talk about
something else.

To the Stars

Yes, the yard is small
but it is yours.
A sanctuary
of sorts
a place for the stars
to rest their wings
hide in shadows
and dance –
as the song goes –
in the moonlight.

The Life and Times of an Iguana

When they kill the sun
I'll know it's over.
Until then
I adapt ...

The Taste of Neon

To walk away
pocket change
rattling
a simple
hangover
and the taste
of neon
forever
on your lips
is a good thing.
I guess.
Luck, if you will.
Then again
if it's her
calling
it's best to let luck
surrender early
and the taste
of the neon
pull you both
back
into the night.

How I Park My Car

No room
for big cars
cigarette smoking women
or bourbon sipping
old men –
the page has turned on us.

Some days
I talk to old men
who don't breathe
gray-skinned women
who only
exhale ...
and anxiety ridden children/boys
who never learned
how to spit properly.
They're all hated
by somebody.
Me too
I guess.

I park my car
anywhere I want
two spaces sometimes.
Go inside, order up a double
straight, on the rocks
sit at the window, sip
think about a different time
a different kind of noise
wonder how the world
got so goddamn quiet.

How a Hitman Eats Spaghetti

I like my marinara
with bow tie pasta.
You don't have to
fuck around
getting it on the fork
just stab it once
and it's done.

Where Things Battle for Their Lives

My world lives purely
in my imagination.
Love, fear, hates
as in plural – more than one –
battle for their lives
there.

My days are their milk
my nights their cradles.
I don't know
if my therapist believes
my stories ...

She wants to know
if I loved my mother.
As if
there is more
to tell.
I finally said yes.
She seemed happy.

The Scales of Worth

Like Red Green says,
"If the women don't find you
handsome
at least
they can find you
handy."

Repaired the upstairs
shower drain –
no more leaks for now.

I go out into the world
fight the battles
for the good of mankind –
come home
and I'm Kae St. Marie's
handyman.

At times
I feel like Picasso
painting the lawn furniture.
The scales of worth
are fickle.

Me and the Moon

The moon is quiet
doesn't want to talk
tonight.
I'll just crawl off
to bed
pretend I don't hear them –
(the wind and the rain)
taunting me.
Wait for another
tomorrow
search the skies
for a whisper
we'll talk then.
Me and the moon.

A Portrait of a Dear Friend

Looking more and more
like the wizard he is –
believe me –
he is.
I've seen
I've heard
I've read his magic.
Besides
he talks to night creatures
and garden fairies.
He knows their names.
I heard he shares his rooms
with a pixie.
She lives in a hole in the wall
behind his favorite painting.
He told a friend
her dust makes his lungs
feel better.
Said
she's nice
to have around.

The Collar

At best we run
with the leash
dragging.

Until they come
to save us
(from ourselves)
and the collar
is again –
tightened.

Nature's Child

The rains woke the river
and the river was pissed.
Threw a raging fit
any three year old
would be proud of.
Beautiful.

Needing Wishes

The wish –
a delicate wrist
small, thin
one deserving
of its own
fragrance
and silver bangles –
worn late
into the morning.
Let them jingle
when she wakes.
There are other things
needing wishes
too.
We'll just start here.
Move on later.

If Only

If only I were an angel
I'd want to stand
wingtip to wingtip
in a circle with you
and the others I've loved.

Make that first
spinning leap
of trust
into a cracking sky.

Parting clouds
until their tears
are shared.

If only we could rinse
one stone
of its sorrow.

We could call ourselves
blessed
and our work
done.
If only ...

A Tip for Hard Times

A bag of thrift-store
paperbacks
one dollar;
twenty – thirty titles.
Cut the covers off
use them for postcards
they're just the right size.
Postage, thirty-five cents.
You may have to
shorten them up
an inch or so
just cut 'em straight.
And try to be selective.
Sending *Mommy Dearest*
for your mother's birthday
could be awkward.

Death of a Swing Set

The guy from the Association
stopped by
asked about the swing set.
Wanted to know
if it was safe.
I said it's a swing set man.
He said it could cause
a hanging
a suicide
something ugly.
Somebody
could get hurt.
Said it's dangerous.
There's no fence
to keep the kids out.
I said it's a swing set man.
It's for the kids.
He said it's got to go.
Gave me 30 days to appeal
before the committee.
We tore it down
burned it in a pile
prayed over its ashes.
Now it's just a scar
in a yard
where kids don't play.

It was the 1950s —

Mine did
always come home dirty.
In the neighborhood
everybody's old man did.

Mom tried to get
the sweat, grime, and tired
out of his shirts —
at least one for Sunday's
early mass.

There was always
a telltale shadow
of a shave needed
another shift waiting
mouths to feed
a lawn to mow
kids to count.

Every once in a while
there was one too many.
Somebody was hungry.
Nobody asked.

He worked the Dodge Plant
drove a truck on the weekends.
There was always
enough.
It was his job.
It was the 1950s —
we were happy.

Concerns for a Spider

The web in the blinds
by my desk
keeps getting bigger.
Don't know
when he works.

I never see
one of those
little wrapped up
mummy things
they keep their prisoners
in
either.

Not sure he's eating
at all
let alone
healthy.

It is the time of year
for the little gray moths
to be out.
I haven't seen
any of their corpses
or even a discarded
wing.

Yes, I am concerned
it's been long enough –
I consider him
(the spider)
a friend.

The Work of Trees

There's a rhythm
to how it moves
when the breeze is gentle
side to side
as if trying
to comfort
an abandoned
dream.

An Oddity

Way back
when I was way younger
riding motorcycles
drinking heavy
and not caring.
I knew a girl who
lived in a teepee
in a campground
over by Pinto Lake,
Watsonville.

The floor was made of
pallets
you had to be careful
where you stepped.
Could twist an ankle.

There was a nasty scar
on the inside of her
right thigh.
Looked like
three or four little
canyons
coming together
deep in the center.
Her skin was smooth
clear – teasing.

She always wore
tight

Daisy Dukes

kept her tan
sharp.

Made it easy to see
even if you weren't looking –
the scar.

Got it from an ex-boyfriend
shot her with a 38 snub nose.
Said it was an accident.

The scar
mostly from taking the bullet out
and putting the steel plates
and screws in
they needed a little more
room
to work.

He got two years
did eighteen months
they don't talk
no more.

It was an oddity
the scar.
She let me touch it
a few times
look close.
It was soft.

Said it tickled
when I did
touch it
and I liked
to touch it.
The scar.

Counting Monsters

When all the monsters
have visited
what else is there
to be frightened of ...

Perhaps not knowing
they have –
unless you've counted.
Even then
you could miss
one or two.

They're
sneaky bastards.
Hiding under beds
in cracks in the walls
even the bottoms
of empty
shot glasses.

That's just a guess
but it does seem
there's always
one more
to deal with.

Unfriended Again

He posted up
he had three poems
in the new issue of
Whatever ...
I commented
"Too bad."

Still Loving Somebody – You
for A.M.

Yeah - it's been a while.
Still missing you
like it was yesterday.

Odd things are happening –
not sure if you'd be smiling
or saying *ah shit* …

I think about you a lot.
Hope you found a
nice corner booth
where it's not too hot

and the barmaid always knows
when it's time
to pour another.

I wish I could say
Happy Birthday
one more time.

I guess those days are gone.
That's it kid.
Still loving you – lots.

Sunrise on a Blind Alley

Getting that feeling – again
shoulders tight
eyes – slits leaking blue
teeth grinding
and just inside the ear
something screams.

We've already gone too far.
Stayed too long
broke all the broken things
turned the sun
into a savage
the moon
a witness
and the sky
a crack above
the rusting fire escapes.

In the morning
when the sun rises
its only reason
to burn another dream
way past ash.

It's sunrise on a blind alley
the windows closed tight
the shades down.
There's no way out.
Everybody's frightened.

Even me.

A Dependable Friend

I've carried a copy
of
Trout Fishing
in America
around
a long time.
The fishhook
a friend gave me
for a book mark
is showing
a bit of rust.
Doesn't hurt nothing
still readable.
Thanks man.

Ambitious Young Men

After you've tried it
and realize
it's a bad idea.
There's either
a lot of talk
in the ER
or evening's cocktails
shared
over warm smiles
and a few laughs
still believing
it could work.

Wishing on a Monarch

Maybe if we close our eyes
tight
hold our breath
till silent
then wish
together
loud –
not too loud though
we'll see another one
before we're gone.

They say
they're endangered.
A lot of days
I feel that way too.

But my list is different.
It has to do
with barmaids
good teeth
silly dreams
and a quiet place
to sit.

And maybe
just one more
seeing
just one more.
Monarch.
Me and you.

A Late Night Report

The Terrace Room
eyes over the far side
of Oakland's lake
lights –
quiver
blink
like they had a secret
they didn't want to keep.

Under the table
stilettos
needing a walk.
She took them
for a spin
drinks and a kiss.

The cabby was blind
the ride home
cheap
the kiss, a bit more.

They both lasted
about the same
(the cab ride and the kiss)
until the stilettos
came off
and the cab's taillights
crossed East 14th.

The moon checked out
early
was a shit of a night.

One of those ...
"take what you brought"
kind of nights.

If you didn't bring anything
nobody –
that's what you went home with
nothing.

The fog
damp
a chill
not a good night for lovers
or strangers.

A few tried
most woke up
lonely.
It was better
that way.
Believe me
I was there.

Then and Now

Ah kid,
old friends and family –
are forever.
Politics aren't enough
to kill the bond.
It's the things you believe in
together
that bind.

Brother Vern, gone now
we'd tangle with them –
often.
Not because we wanted to,
but because we had to.
It was different.
we were there – part of it.

He'd tell me
It doesn't mean nothing
until the blood soaks in –
then it's yours.
Wanted to know
Was that something we needed to do.
I'd tell him, yeah.

We'd go down to the Crow's Nest
the Yacht Harbor, Santa Cruz
order up New Yorks
and Harvey Wallbangers
act like we had money.

Talk about getting Kae St. Marie's
52 Chevrolet back on the road.

It was 1969
she liked the salad bar
it was new
we were young.

Private Dreams

A bit of magic
the quiet
a peaceful place
to drift away
and a few
secrets.
Flying helps
but not always
necessary.

Searching for Two, Finding Three

There are things
two things
I've ever wanted:
To be left alone
and a good death.
If love finds me
and it has
a few times
that would be nice
too.

Another Tomorrow

Never.
Never –
take an old man's
tools.
They should always
be the last to go.
Well after him.
When they do
it's done.

No knuckles
scraped.
Nothing
for old hands
to push, pull, turn
swing –
to hold on to.
No lessons to pass.

Even in rust
they keep what was
alive.

Without them
there's no wish
to bless
another tomorrow.

Keeping Dogs

She likes to have a dog
in the house.

Says she needs
someone
something
to listen
to talk to
to sit with
and hold.

I told her,
I'm here
for you baby.

She just smiled.

We Get By

Once –
straight, tall
and handsome.
Walks with a cane
these days.
She still knows how
to flash a smile though.
Me
a bit more slumped.
Not as strong
as I used to be
but still got the
power
to hold the door
push her chair in.
The rent's paid
laundry folded.
Now and then
there's a bit extra
for the movies
a bag of popcorn
a cold drink.
For the most part
we get by.

Trying for Human

Forgiveness?
I've asked.

I've done everything
wrong —
everything.
I'm guilty.

I give up
don't forgive me
ever.

These days
I find
it better
to bleed
together:
heart
mind
soul.

No need to talk about
my tragedies.
I'm sure
you've experienced
your own.

If my name's
not mentioned
that's good enough.

If it is
you should have
stayed away ...
Remember – I told you.

Filling Time and Gone

Daughters grow up
move away
call home.

Sons grow up
move away
get called home.

It's the nature
of families.

There's a meal
cold drinks
talk about
flawed memories
goodbyes.

And out there
somewhere
a final call
waiting.

A generation
fades –
and time finds
someone new
to help it fill
the cracks
of who we are.

Scary People and Madmen
- The Death of a Robot, for Trump 6/21/2019

It appears
our robot
has met an unfortunate end
while flying over
the Strait of Hormuz.

The office staff is still playing
Hide-and-Seek
with the Nuclear Button
and it seems the president's
received
another call
from Putin.
For that, we should pray.
Be grateful.

There really is
nothing else
to say
when dealing
with scary people
and madmen.

Sunday's Family Potluck

The gravy
is weak
and the bourbon
thin.
Still, both help
to cut the taste
of Uncle Frank's
scalloped potatoes.

Sub-Allergies

They don't make
my eyes water
or things like that.

It's just
I don't really care
for them.

So I stay away
avoid their
company –
don't pick up
the phone or
answer
emails.

If someone
mentions
they haven't been
able
to get through –
well ...
you know
I'm busy.

Private Things

The night's feeling empty.
There's a wound here
I wish I could fix.
But she likes her sorrow —
won't let it happen.
She's not mine to repair.
Not that I've truly
tried.

I don't look like
him
sound like
him
or burn like
him.
Just an old man
turning
chrome
in the beard.

All I know about love
is:
Sometimes
you have to forgive
somebody
before you can
move on.
And she isn't ready.

There it is —
a tall, skinny, tattooed

girl
heading west

alone
back to the coast
her safe place
waiting.

She's bringing
moments
to drift away in
a car packed
with ash, dreams
memories
and private things
not
to be talked about.

The Wait

It's green out there
just green
lots of green.
Beautiful
though —
green.

A flower
would be nice.
Any color
you pick.
Maybe next year?
We'll have to wait.

Reporting Secrets

All of what I am
is there
in hidden places.

Find them, my secrets
and you'll know
why I choose
not to tell.

From My Hands to Yours

It was once filled
with magic and dreams
enough for a lifetime
there could be a few left
if you look hard enough.

The tool box
sixty pounds
of mostly iron.
Paid the rent
for a lot of years.
Forty at least.

If you find this note
you're probably
cleaning out the garage
if you keep anything
keep this
the tools, the box.

Put it in a corner
on a stack of newspapers
in your living room.
A conversation piece.

If anyone asks
tell them
It was once filled
with magic and dreams.
Tell them you heard
a lot of them came true.
Tell them it's yours now.

A Wish for a Friend on Her Birthday

Happy Birthday kid.
May the wonder
and craziness
never end
and you
forever
be part of it.

That's a nice
wish.
It feels good
making it.
For you.

Dark Skies, Turkey Vultures, And Somebody's Uncle

On hot days
the Turkey Vultures
turn the sky dark
circling the house.
Somebody
could have died here
but it would have been
a while ago.

We bought the place
from an old guy and his wife
who inherited it
from his dead uncle.
The neighbors said
he was
peculiar.

We never got the details
on how the uncle
passed.
If it was an ugly deal
they did a good job
cleaning up the mess.

We leave the back
kind of in shambles.
Oh, I mow it down
per the fire code
but I'm not about
to go around
digging holes

planting things
cultivating.

There could be a pet
cemetery
back there
or a dismembered
ex-wife
down a few feet.

The Turkey Vultures
know something.
It's their secret
we'll leave it at that.

Another Goodbye

They took a tooth
today.
A molar
way back
in the back.
At my age
I guess I can
afford
to lose one.
Still it was an old
friend.
Lots of red meat
bacon
sourdough
dipped in blood
egg yoke
bourbon
and Harvey Wallbangers
pasted its way.
My guess –
a couple hundred pounds
worth.
It was a good tooth.
I'll miss it.

Heart-worn

Got an old woman
says she loves me.
Got the place
it's mostly ours
try to mind
my own business
it never works.

There's always somebody
wanting to know something.
I generally tell them
the wrong thing
even if it's right.

People should have signs
on strings
hanging around their necks
saying
this is what I want to hear.

Make it easy on an old man.
I don't want to fight
no more.
Not at my age.
But I still carry a knife
there's a ball peen hammer
in the car
and a revolver
under the seat.
Just in case.
The other option
is to just leave it alone.

The knuckles ache
back too.
It takes a bit
to get out of the chair.

I'm worn out
tired
even the heart hurts.
Too much stuff.
Seems I'm just
hanging around
waiting for the good.

I get up in the morning
and it's scrambled eggs
and peppers
tomato juice, Tabasco
lemon
and salt.
Sometimes, if I sleep in
it's soup.

I'll ask her
what're you doing today –
baby.
She'll pour the coffee
tell me
every time
like it's the first time:
Loving you
and that heart-worn
old soul
that keeps you
hanging around.

To Dance

I don't dance
with the angels
anymore.
Not unless
they like bourbon –
Harvey Wallbangers
or when the money's
tight –
beer.

I dance with them –
the girls
who raise their arms up
high
make fists
point at things
that aren't there
and laugh out loud.

The ones whose hips
pulse
when the music's – hot.

I'll dance
with them.
The girls –
whose bits and pieces
have their own kind of smiles –
know when to show
their teeth.

Know how to ask
the morning
your name.

How I Heard It

Rich Bethany —
a friend
hung himself
up in Oregon
in an apple tree
of all goddamn things.

They said
it was over a girl.
Could have been.
I always thought
he had sharper teeth
than that.

But I do know
there are times
when the weight
of the world
is balanced
on one
"I love you."

And when she takes it back
everything under your
feet crumbles.

An apple tree?
I guess
as good as any
when it's time
to call it quits.

Dust Bowl Photos

If you ever noticed
moms, dads
the old folks
all looking down.

Only the kids
looking out
of those photos
into your eyes.

Some saying
just give me a knife
a piece of bread.
Some, just waiting to die.

It's what happens
when times get ugly
people get ugly.
It's easy to make days
hurt.

I remember
back in the fifties
my grandma would say
all that's on the plate
is all there is.
Don't waste nothing.

She'd say
if you're still hungry
sneak off
to Mr. Johnson's place.

Half a block up Melrose.
His peach tree's
coming in.
Hanging over the sidewalk
don't break no branches
don't take none to waste.
Other folks might be
hungry too.

If he comes out
yelling
tell him Mrs. Pressey
says
thank you
and run like hell.

Walking into Loneliness

All those first times
I was scared then.
Now
looking at the last times
I'm scared again.

It would be nice
a little silly
even
but nice
if there's someone
there
to hold my hand
when my crossing
is close.

Talk the cheap talk
the easy stuff
the lies
about beauty
love
and missing you.

Maybe a middle aged
woman
nice hair
a little salt
good teeth
and a smile
No church breath.
Just someone

who knows
how to walk you
out

into the field
tall grass
butterflies
and red winged
black birds.

Tells you it's time
to let go.
Tells you
you're safe.
Now.
Forever.

And makes you
believe it.

Old Poets

An old friend
got knocked over
in NOLA.
Hell
what's an old poet
got?
Empty pockets.
They cleaned him
out.
Took it
all.
At the airport
they gave him
a hard
time.
What the hey –
man.
Rock stars
get inlaid
pistols
and thugs
so they can act
tough.
Old poets
it's a hangover
and a long ride
home –
empty
and alone.

Different Kinds of Friends

I've seen a horse's face
in the leaves of a tree ...
between the blinds
peeking out
a hot
end of summer
day.
Other things
too.
Real and imaginary.

I don't respond
to the neighbor's screams
anymore.
She gave me a code
word, for help.
I didn't tell her
I hear things too.
Real and imaginary.

It's been happening
a while now.
I don't talk about it much.
If the wrong people
find out
they might want to
take my:
driver's license
pistol
and kitchen knives.

Or even
try to cure me
of the problem.

If it is
a problem.
I wouldn't like that.
It's nice not being
lonely.
Only scares me
sometimes.

The Lucky One

It's late
time for bed.
I got monsters
waiting for me.
I wish they'd love
somebody else.
But, I'm always
the lucky one.
Who do you thank
for that?

Bloody August

9/1/2019

YESTERDAY –
It was YESTERDAY,
for Christ's sake!
People shot
people killed
Odessa, Texas.

Yesterday they talked –
said all the right things
showed the pictures
on the TV
and offered condolences.
Today – nothing.

Bloody August
moves on
barbecue,
cold drinks
and watermelon
for the kids.

September steps in
Labor Day weekend
campaign speeches
empty promises
funeral arrangements
to be made.

Dressing for Drinks and a Movie

Just wear the pearls.
You don't need
nothing else
baby.
Not with me.
Just the pearls.

Realizing Brautigan

Punching in
the time clock
hanging there
gray.
Why gray?

And me
lining up
my card
dropping it in
and that clunk.

Pulling
my hand back
feeling it hit
me in the chest
as if saying
you're mine now.

All that I am:
Eight hours
ten hours
twelve
sometimes a double –
forgets about – me.

It's the machines' time
now.
The machines who
watch over us
in "loving grace."

Traveling with Ghosts

A bigger suitcase
would be nice.

Shaky Old Men
and Upscale Joints

He held his drink
with two hands.
One for the glass
the other
for the straw —
never raised it
off the table.

When they brought
the second
he had to upcycle
the straw.

Move it from
one glass
to the other.
The cheap
bastards.

The Purpose
of the Little Garage

Been building a
little garage
in the back.

Actually
it's a little room
with a big door
a window
and a little
door
that open
to the world.

I wish to sit there
someday
sip my bourbon
enjoy the rocks
out front
the movement of time
and the quiet.

Not the silence.
Silence is scary
but the quiet –

The quiet
is when time
holds you
peacefully
in its hands.

The birds, bugs
and other things
and sometimes
nothing – stop by.

In a whisper
I'll wish them well
offer a cold drink
a place to sit
and a little time
in the quiet.

Amazing Things about Bugs

Last night
in bed
a bug
one of those
shiny black
long legged beasts
you find in the garden
was walking up
my arm.
The hairy side.

When I went to
brush it off
my hand went
right through it.
Like a shadow.
Then it was back.
When I blinked
it was gone –
again.

Amazing –
I didn't know
bugs
could do that.

Drinking with Saints

Half a quart of bourbon
or whatever they call it
these days.
I can do it in a night
still be comfortable
with who I am.

Maybe lie
a little bit.
Maybe not.
It's my time.
I never asked
anybody
to talk.

There are secrets
to tell.
How much ugly
we've got.
A lot.
What else are they
going to take?
Sooner or later –
all of it.
Tonight
I'm drinking
fuck it.

You want to talk
get loud.
Otherwise, kiss the saints

ask them
him or her
to forgive the interruption.

Me – leave me
to the bourbon.

A Place to Suffocate

It's okay
until the rats
start eating
the pigeons
and the brave
start to fear
sleeping alone.

The city
has its own
scary places.
Doesn't it?

A long list
of disturbing
things –
add to it
if you need to.

And don't let the cat
in the house
when the baby
has milk
on its breath.
Mysterious things
could happen.

Gardening by Starlight

It's not as quiet as you
might think.
The garden creatures
like to chat.
The reptiles
field mice
night birds
beetles, bugs and spiders.

Their languages are a bit
troublesome
can be hard to grasp.
I found it best
to keep a distance
smile and wave.

It's often wise
to let them
go about their
business
finish their work
before inviting
conversation.

If not
you could be up
all night
listening to
the complaints
of interruption.

The little beasts
can be very pushy
when imposed on.

Moving Out

The tenants
poke holes in the walls
to hang family portraits
and other heavy things.
He plugs them
with cigarette butts
and white toothpaste
a generous amount
so he doesn't
have to paint.

The Imposition of Guilt

I don't know if I told you —
The best way to find
if a rule
truly has merit —
is to use it.

At my age I find little reason
to test rules.
I ignore them.

If my infraction is too serious
to overlook
I accept my guilt
and simply ask for mercy.

Forgiveness is for
the innocent.

A New Used Hat

Reading the obituaries
a habit —
might need to rent a room
sometime.
Pick up a car cheap.
See how fast the guy's stuff
shows up
on the garage sale list.
Could be a deal to be had.

No sentiment here
the guy's dead
he needs me
like I need him.
Could be a buck to be made.

Memories, they slip away.
Sure, they'll talk about him
next Christmas
maybe his birthday.
Truth is, he'll drift away
like we all do.
But I'll remember him
long after they've finished
the pumpkin pie.

Going through his stuff
finding his hat.
It's hard to find a good used hat
my size — seven and five-eights.
When you do
grab it up, be thankful.

I do wish his
was a little fuller in the brim
and the color leaned a little more
toward burgundy.

But hey, I wear it
and now and then
somebody will ask
want to know
where I got it.
I tell 'em
from a guy I met
in the newspaper.

The Truth about Love Stories

They all end
in tragedy.

Sooner or later
someone dies.

Before that
it's just an ugly end.

Two people
alone
to wonder.

A Little Something for the Dogs

Christ, I've outlived so many.
All good friends
except Floyd and Sonny
they were just assholes.
.

I'll have to leave a little something
in the will
for Rose and Miss Parker.

Find someone else
for them to love
to look after –
sleep with.

When Love Died

They filled the piano
with flowers
and let it rot ...

Disneyland Vacation Summary – (Millennium Falcon: Smuggler's Run)

Kae St. Marie yelled at me
twice
for crashing the Millennium Falcon –
twice ...
"Hit the thrusters, hit the thrusters –
the blue button – dammit ..."
Even the little kids yelled at me.
It was terrible.
I left the bridge
head hung
in shame.

Don Quixote's Last Battle

There was a guy with Alzheimer's
at the reading the other night.
I helped his daughter
get him to the stage for open mic.
Actually we just sat him in a chair
and moved the mic to him.
He said he was from
a little college town
in upstate Massachusetts.
He talked about his son
and how he thought
we needed more poets
in the world.
He rattled on for a bit
mentioned his daughter.
Pointed to a stranger
across the room
said there she is now.
The daughter said
I'm over here Dad.
He smiled, said
she gets around.
I helped her get him
back to their table.
In the jumble of all he was
he asked how he did –
Great man ... you were great.
He said
you know Robert Lowell
he's pretty flat.
Don Quixote's saber rattled
one last time.

Jane – even after she went crazy ...

Hey kid
you never call
you never write –
not even a postcard ...
but yeah
I still love you –
think about you
now and then
look for things
you've left behind
in those old haunts.
A picture, a scent
a note on the wall.
I miss you.
Here it is your birthday
again
and I'm celebrating
alone ...
a glass of beer
a shot of bourbon.
It doesn't warm me
the way you do.
But hey kid
nothing does.
Until we're close again
Happy Birthday –
miss you
terribly.

Once We Were Kids

The sister-in-law
not doing good.
In the ICU.
She's still in the game
but they told her
not to expect
much
or too long.

The nurse comes in
sounds optimistic
while telling the
ugly things.
Everything's
shutting down.

She doesn't know
about the good stuff
the crazy-fun stuff
when we were all
younger
a bit wild
and dying seemed so
far away.

Well
it's on us now.
Her kids –
worried about their share.
Ours, tell stories and smile.
Kae St. Marie

carrying a little more weight
on her shoulders.
The world just got
a bit heavier.

Never Less than Harmful

Every night
the hand of God
is there
on my chest
threatening
to crush me.

Feeling every weight
of every challenge
every loss
that didn't have to be.

Arms outstretched
I keep the world
just that far away.

The only safe place
is alone.
Even there
I'm haunted.

Finding Forever

The mid thirties
until the late fifties
are the greatest years
for the greatest adventures.

I hope you haven't missed
yours
or let the small dreams
be washed away by time.
Those lives
are to be lived
just once.
They're important.
Very important.

There are no
do-overs
no ball two
no second roll of the dice.
Just the discovery:

*To leave no monument
to the past –
is the greatest monument
to the future.*

You're Dead

There's a good chance
a very good chance
I could kill you
this evening.
No, it wouldn't be
an easy thing.
I would expect you
to offer a good fight.
Then that moment
when it all changes
and you're dead.
I wake up
in the morning
tired
a few bruises I can't explain
and never
hear from you
again.
Ever.
You're dead.

A Friend Reads Siddhartha

A friend sent a note
said she was away
on a trip.
Took Siddhartha
to read again.
It had been fifty years.

Hesse –
someone I've always
loved.

I replied
Siddhartha
an old friend
from what seemed
troubled times –
and here we are
again.
In those times.

Hope
you enjoy it.

Once at the Edge of the Ocean

(for the grieving)

In the sand
a half gone paper sack
an empty half pint
label eaten away.
Somebody was warm
for a little while.
It doesn't matter
who.
They were just
warm
for a little while.

The Distance Between Us

(for the sick)

They say
if you die from it
you die alone.
If I had any left
I'd pray for you.
I don't.
All there is –
a wish.
A wish
to wish you well.
A wish for another
tomorrow.

Falling Stars
(for the dead)

Piling all the falling stars
in the backyard for now.
Don't know what I'll do
with them.
There are so many.
No –
I don't remember
their names
faces
or numbers
just that once
they were here
with me
shining
so bright.

Learning to Fly

Don't know
about
heading south
with the geese
the height
might scare me
or flying with the
Sand Cranes –
all that noise.
Perhaps the Monarchs
but with such tight flutters
the banging of wings
slapping, and the pushing.
I'm not good in crowds.
I could clean up my resume.
Ask the angels to take a
vote.
Who knows
I could get lucky.
Anything
beats stepping off
the ledge.

Believing in a Troubled God

We pray on Wednesday.
The same night they pull
the lotto.

The rest of the week
at the dinner table
we make wishes
for something better.

When Wednesday comes
we pray –
our wishes come
true.

On Thursday
we make new wishes.

Dogs and Reptiles
Spring 2020

Had to go out last week
get the dogs their
rattlesnake vaccinations.
Lockdown or not,
the snakes are still out.

In Dust and Ash

In death
I wish to be cremated.
Trying to convince
Kae St. Marie of the same
but still, after leaving the church
so many years back
she carries the Catholic belief
of returning to the earth.

It would be nice though
our ghosts together
dancing
in the evenings
slow
holding each other
whispering warm whispers
across the other's ear –
like we did
in the beginning.

Lighting Cigarettes and Saying No

She has a Zippo
and knows how to use it.
Lights her own
cigarettes
the occasional candle
for an ex-lover
and the stove
when it's cold.
Flicks it open
and closed
when nervous.
Keeps the edge
of the lid
sharp
good for drawing
blood
when the answer is
no.
Clamp it on
and squeeze.

Thinking about Stuff

It's quiet tonight.
Everyone you love
gone to sleep
left you
to it.

So you just think about
the stuff
that you think about
now and then
when you're alone.

You know
it all means nothing.

Less than nothing

but it's yours
to worry about –
so you do.

Miles Away

Knuckles hurt
back hurts too.
Everything fucking hurts.
It's who I am.

Then there's the cute picture
on a Christmas card
Kae St. Marie and the family
me –
looking innocent.

There are times
when all you can do
is look
smile
and let the wish
take you miles away
from who you are.
While trying
not to blink.

The Lockdown
2020

The safest
I've ever felt.
Period.

Happily Ever After

I'm pushing 72
Kae St. Marie, 70.

All we wanted
was to live
happily ever after.

But this fucking POTUS –
Trump
is just a dream killer.
Why?

I don't wish him any harm
but if he should die
with a smoldering
chunk of charcoal
up his ass –

I could live
with that.

The Stranger

The old man's
just a picture
kept in a trunk.
That's all I know
of him.

Sure, I make up stories.
He never gets to be the hero.
I don't remember him
that way.

Just a stranger
coming and going
never said much
and when he did
it was made of
disappointment.

What People Eat

My mother was Irish
we ate potatoes
a lot of potatoes.
I still do.

Lying To a Bill Collector

Final Notice
Bill Gainer
Democratic Membership: Pending

I know Barack
has emailed me
and Carville
and Hillary
Adam Schiff
Mayor Pete
Barney Frank
and a few others.

Look, the wife is on the couch
coughing up blood.
I'm trying to stretch every
penny
for the morphine.
She's trying to hold out
until the election
doesn't want to leave
the world like this.
Can you give me a break?
I just need a little time ...
That's all
a little time.

The Focused Beatle

He was cool until he spoke
then he became Richard Starkey.
The dumb Beatle.

Not really a feat for this guy.
Sharp suit, pointed shoes
tie and collar
flashing peace symbols.

He always seemed to be
just
hanging around.
Collecting what was his
looking cool.

Every once in a while
they'd let him sing.
The rest of the time
he was just quiet
trying to keep the beat
focused.

Breakfast

Waffles and jam.
The waffles give the jam
texture.
The jam – the waffles
sweetness.
Now
to get the jar open
before
things get cold.

The Truth about Wild Dogs

These flare-ups come around
every now and then.
Everybody gets worked up
buys a bunch of guns, locks
and plywood
starts walking the kids to school.
Someone gets hurt
broken, frightened
left with, "Why?"
Demands are made
committees are formed,
they have a few meetings
blab it up
it all means something
to somebody.
Nothing gets done,
it fades away
the rhetoric remains
the uneasy normal
returns
and all gets quiet
for a few more years.
Then it comes around again.
The people in the high houses
are just trickier,
stronger,
and more insincere
than ever imagined.
So, we the people
pop our heads up
every once in a while

scare the hell out of everybody
get loud
hope the uneasy lies
are true
and like a whack-a-mole
get beat back down.
And those like you and me
continue the good fight
until the promises are kept.
Till then
we remain wild dogs –
showing our teeth now and then
growling low
licking our wounds.

The Art of Growing Cacti

My cactus has become a monster.
I have no idea how to prune it
or even if I'm supposed to.
It had flowers this year
for like three days.
I think it loves me,
but not that much.

Waiting for the Rain

Too long
in the good fight.

Wouldn't think old age
could carry so much pain
or a heart could be
so heavy
waiting for the rain
the cool
the lonely hours.

Checking the mail
the newspaper
they'll call
when they need
another body
to stand the line.

It's funny
how the enemy becomes
just another pair of eyes
like your eyes
looking back
holding ground
wishing as you wish
their truth
would become
your truth
and the rain
would send them home.

Counting Kills

I've never thought
of a balloon
as a toy ...
entertainment maybe.
The best part of which
is the popping
and sometimes
waiting for one
to disappear
into the clouds.
Wondering
if an airplane
ever hit one
and if the pilot
remembering the war
still paints insignias
across his fuselage.
Counting
kills.

A Quick Turnaround

Some guy
sent a friend request.
I said okay.

Just to be safe
I decided to send him
a message
"You better not be
one of those
Commie rats."

I guess he was.

A Drive to the Coast

We visited the seashore
brought back
seashells, a smooth rock
pieces of colored glass
and a sand dollar.
All once alive
now just
tiny corpses
to be collected
on the window sill.
Memories
of a day at the beach.

A Lonely Angel

Trying to fly
without wings
a fool's game.

I guess it's curiosity
keeping me here
waiting for the one
right thing
to lift me.

In the faces
on the streets
few possess grace
most fear
when they glance
it's a lonely glance.

As they walk by
I see no wings
and no one
flies
without wings.

The Package

Before me
the old man owned a gas station
over on the Bay Shore.
I don't know exactly where.
I've seen the pictures
him dressed in white
a dark jacket
a Derby hat.
Bettie, my Mom,
told me he was robbed once.
After that he carried
a set of brass knuckles
in one pocket
and a small pistol in the other.
He sold the station
a few years later.
Then the war.
After –
he went to work at the Dodge plant
until it closed
ran a trucking company
until it killed him.
It was a nice funeral
a couple of his sisters
came out from West Virginia.
Friends and family
quiet talk
the drinking at the house
wasn't too bad.
Driving the aunts to the airport
the soft weeping
and polite goodbye lies.

A few months later
got a package in the mail
heavier than it looked
the brass knuckles
and a pistol
a few loose bullets
and a note from Bettie
Just in case
you ever buy
a gas station.

For the Boy

Two girls and a boy.
The boy, our youngest,
had two cancer scares.
He's survived both.
Still, we've learned things
we never wanted to know.
Things that take
you to your knees.
He still lives
a bit on the wild side.
I guess that's just
something else
in the blood.

Five Love Letters

I could have written
a thousand.
Decided on five
to the women I've loved.
Mail them
after I'm gone.

If you get one
thank you.
If not
know
you were always
a wish.

You could have brought
a lot of joy.
Maybe you did
to someone else.
I'm glad for him.

Maybe it's because
I never asked
so you never did.
Maybe because
I scared you.
Never meant to.

Five is good.
A nice font
a simple note

*I have always
loved you —*

You might wonder
why
why now
why didn't I say something
before.

Maybe because you were there
and that was all I needed.
Besides, what else
is a surprise for
if not
a goodbye tear.

The American Poem

If it is four
five, six pages
long
it is for someone else
to read.

I have never taken
that long
to fall in love.

A line or two
to set the hook.
You can fill in the rest
over dinner.

The Girl with Long Fingers

Just watching her
kissing the berry juice
from the tips of her fingers
is enough –
almost.

At Almost 75
10.10.2023

I was planning
on going out
quietly.
But now the bastards
are planning
to blow the world up –
again.

Thinking about
getting a trumpet
playing it late
at night –
loud.
Waking the neighbors
up.
Letting them know
I'm not in this thing
alone.

The Movies

Black and white
all the color
needed
to fill a dream ...

She Can Fix an Ocean

Slid the empty across the bar.
Said, "The tide's out kid."
She said, "Don't worry Love
I can fix an ocean –
all it takes
is a bit of ice
a clean glass
and a smile
from you."

A Little Smoke

We both were breathing heavy
she grabbed a cigarette
from the nightstand.

The fire from her match
laid a shadow on her face
the smoke gave the night reason.

She asked if I wanted a hit
pushed the sheets down
said the night is ours.

I took the cigarette
said
I was hoping.

She blew a little smoke.
It was
beautiful.

Mexico

They're playing guitars
down in Mexico.
Makes me feel like
dancing
maybe singing.
You sing?
You want to go?

Ain't got no passport.
How about El Paso?
I know a girl down there
used to be an attorney
civil rights and stuff.
She keeps dogs.
Might keep us
a day or two.

I don't know if she sings
but I have heard her hum
under her breath
beautiful
sad though.
She lost a man
a few years back.
Pulls on her.
She's still sweet
especially with those
dogs.

Well kid
what do you think – go?
El Paso
it's as close as we can get.

Bill Gainer is a storyteller, humorist, poet, and a maker of mysterious things. He earned his BA from St.Mary's College, and his MPA from the University of San Francisco. He is the publisher of the PEN Award winning R. L. Crow Publications, and was the host of Red Alice's Poetry Emporium (Sacramento, CA). Gainer is internationally published, and known across the country for giving legendary fun filled performances. His work is not for sissies. Visit him in his books, at his personal appearances, or at his website: billgainer.com.

This project was made possible, in part, by generous support from the Osage Arts Community.

Osage Arts Community provides temporary time, space and support for the creation of new artistic works in a retreat format, serving creative people of all kinds — visual artists, composers, poets, fiction and nonfiction writers. Located on a 152-acre farm in an isolated rural mountainside setting in Central Missouri and bordered by ¾ of a mile of the Gasconade River, OAC provides residencies to those working alone, as well as welcoming collaborative teams, offering living space and workspace in a country environment to emerging and mid-career artists. For more information, visit us at www.osageac.org

Osage Arts Community

Milton Keynes UK
Ingram Content Group UK Ltd.
UKHW041943131124
451149UK00005B/478